the

gr

wedding

the essentials for your role

confetti.co.uk

An Hachette Livre UK Company
www.hachettelivre.co.uk
First published in 2004 by Octopus Publishing Group,
2–4 Heron Quays, London E14 4JP
www.octopusbooks.co.uk
3 5 7 9 10 8 6 4 2

ISBN: 978-1-84091-363-7
A CIP catalogue record for this book is available
from the British Library.
Printed and bound in China
Publishing Director Lorraine Dickey
Senior Editor Katey Day
Assistant Editor Sybella Marlow
Art Director Chi Lam
Designer Jeremy Tilston
Assistant Production Controller Natalie Moore

Contents

THE GROOM'S WEDDING

So you're going to do it – take the step into the big M. If that weren't nerve-wracking enough, there are 101 things to think about to make sure the path to the altar is a smooth one.

INTRODUCTION

Whether it's the first time or the third time
of pledging your troth, whether you're
planning to propose or she's already
popped the question, this book is
designed to give you, the groom, all
the advice and ideas you'll need
to make sure you get hitched
without a hitch.

The ring

Traditionally the man pays for the ring, and
one popular guideline (admittedly
perpetrated by the diamond industry)
is that it should cost him a month's salary.
It should be left to the individual to decide
whether that's net or gross!

The ring

Planning a surprise? Be sneaky and check your girlfriend's ring size by 'borrowing' one of her other rings, or wrap a piece of string around her finger while she's asleep and marking it where it joins. Make sure you get the right finger (third finger of the left hand, i.e. one in from the little one).

Just in case...

Always keep the receipt. If she hates it, or says no, or if you ever need to make an insurance claim, you might need that receipt. Insure your ring as soon as possible, just in case. If you plan to pop the question abroad, make sure it's covered by your travel insurance, in case it drops from your pocket on the way to that deserted coral island.

The proposal

Proposing on the radio, in the bath, at work, up the Eiffel Tower or floating in a hot-air balloon over the Serengeti sipping Champagne: there are a million ways to propose. Whatever your chosen approach, remember:

Proposal tips

Do it for the right reasons
Try not to embarrass her
The more romantic the better, and
KISS – Keep it Simple and Sincere!

Getting Pa's permission

In a recent poll, a full 65 per cent answered 'yes' to the question, 'Should potential grooms ask permission from the bride's father?' It seems that seeking the permission of the bride's father (or mother, or both) is alive and well. But is it for you?

Pros and cons

Pros: an in-law is for life, not just for your wedding day. So it could be a good diplomatic move to get you off on the right foot.

Cons: it might upset your intended. If you have even the slightest inkling that she feels the whole concept is outdated and belongs to a less egalitarian era, don't even think about it!

Telling everyone

It's usually best to tell close family first before spreading the news far and wide. How you do this is up to you — phone, email, in person or even over the tannoy at the supermarket.

Announcements

Wedding announcements are traditionally placed in the local and national newspapers by the bride's parents. But you can place announcements yourself, or follow the modern route that is becoming popular and announce it online, using an Internet service such as Confetti.

Setting the date

You may have a specific date in mind, or you may be quite open. Either way, it's worth bearing in mind that it's often easier to find available dates for venues, registrars etc. outside the traditional wedding season (May to September).

What to think about

Planning a wedding also takes a fair amount of time and effort, so unless you are going for a really simple event or have lots of help available, leave yourself a reasonable period of time. The average engagement nowadays lasts 19 months.

Announcing the date

Try and be as sensitive as possible when setting the date. For instance, picking the week before the bride's sister is due to get married could cause some serious family upset.

Remember, don't announce the date, print invitations or make arrangements until you have received written commitment from the venue and the celebrant.

Who pays for the wedding?
Nowadays, the cost of even the most
modest wedding can be astronomical.
In fact, the average Confetti user's
wedding costs £15,000! Although
traditionally the bride's parents pay
for most of the wedding, more
and more couples are now
paying for their own
big day.

THE GROOM'S WEDDING

Whose responsibilities?

The groom is traditionally responsible for certain expenses. These include:

Ceremony and music - £200

The bride's wedding ring - £200

Transport - £250

The first night hotel - £200

The honeymoon - £2100

These are average costs compiled from the budgets of Confetti users.

The price of love

For more information on average costs and
for a free budget planner to keep tabs on
the expense, visit www.confetti.co.uk

Cutting costs

Think about what you actually want at your wedding, and what you think you could do without (for instance, if you don't like fruitcake, there's probably little point in splashing out on an amazing cake!).

More hints:

Save on transport costs by borrowing from a mate with a flash car.

Hire outfits rather than buying them.

How to make savings

Weekday weddings are often considerably cheaper. Encourage the bride to choose flowers that are in season.

And, finally, don't forget to take out insurance. If the marquee blows away or you have to cancel through illness, it won't take away the pain of disappointment but it will help the pain in your wallet.

THE GROOM'S WEDDING

Who's the best man?

In a nutshell, he organizes the stag night, accompanies the groom to the ceremony, brings the rings to the ceremony, introduces the speeches at the wedding breakfast and makes the best speech himself.

Best man for the job?

The best man is meant to perform a supportive role, and not add to the pressure. So avoid asking someone who is too busy or unreliable, or who has had a previous relationship with the bride.

Two's the best man?

If the groom can't, or doesn't want to, decide between two friends, or one can't make the stag party and the other can't make the wedding, it's fine to have two best men. If both are present, they can stand up front with you during the ceremony, and you can divvy up the day's responsibilities as follows:

Dividing the responsibilities

One brings the rings, the other acts
as toastmaster for the speeches,
cake cutting etc.

One is master of ceremonies for the day,
the other makes the speech.

They make a joint best man speech and
hand over one ring each.

Who's the best woman?

If your best mate/best choice for best man is a woman, it's advisable to make sure that you and the bride are in agreement over this one, as it's just possible she might not be keen on another woman at the altar on her big day. If she has no reservations, then go right ahead.

Choosing the ushers

This is a much easier job, and is a nice honour to bestow on friends or brothers. There's no rule as to how many you should have, but as their main role is to organize the guests at the ceremony, a smaller venue will suggest fewer ushers, and a larger one more.

Getting married abroad

If the idea of getting married with the Caribbean sand between your toes or the Spanish sun on your back appeals to you, then you'll be pleased to know that getting married abroad is often considerably less expensive and less hassle than getting married at home.

Before you check in

Before you book the first tickets out of here, there are two things to consider. First, check you will be able to fulfil all the legal and residential requirements of your chosen destination. Second, check you won't be hurting anyone's feelings – often family can feel excluded from weddings abroad.

Legal checklist

To be legally married in the UK, you must fulfil these requirements:

You and your partner must be at least 16 years old. (In England and Wales, if either party is under 18, written consent to the marriage must be obtained from the parents or legal guardian.)

You must not be closely related.

Legal checklist

The marriage must take place in premises where marriage can be legally solemnized. These include register offices, premises that have been given a civil licence by the local authority, parish churches of the Church of England and other churches that have been registered by the register general for worship and marriage.

There are exceptions for military marriages and for those who are housebound.

Legal checklist

The ceremony must take place in the
presence of a superintendent registrar,
a registrar or an authorized person.
The ceremony must take place between
8am and 6pm (with the exception of the
Jewish religion and the Society of Friends).

Two witnesses must be present to
witness the ceremony.

You must both be free and
eligible to marry.

Legal checklist

Legal requirements vary for marriages abroad, so be sure you know exactly what you need to provide. However, the good news is that if your marriage is considered legal in the country in which it was contracted, then it will be recognized in the UK.

Fight the flab

If you're not quite at your fighting weight,
then what better incentive for getting
into shape than looking good on your
wedding day. Remember to go about it
sensibly — you don't want to overdo
it and look haggard and grey in
the photos.

Fight the flab

If you are planning to lose a fair amount
of weight – or bulk up the muscles
to impress your bride on your
honeymoon – then remember to
factor this in when deciding when
to hire or buy your suit.

Good hair day

Considering a change of hairstyle?
It may take two or three cuts to get there,
so see your hairdresser at least three
months before the wedding. Try to resist
the temptation to surprise your bride by
turning up at the altar having shaved your
beard off, grown a moustache or dyed
your hair. It could all go horribly wrong.

A close shave

If you're prone to five o'clock shadow or you're particularly nervous, then you may want to consider getting a professional shave on the morning of your wedding. Apart from anything else, it is a wonderfully relaxing experience.

Man-icure

A manicure a day or two before the big day
will leave your nails cleaner than you've
ever seen them, which is especially wise
if you're doing the ring thing. Don't be
shy – everyone's at it these days!

How to tie ties

The following are simple instructions
for three classic tie styles.

The Bow Tie

The Bow Tie

The Bow Tie should be tied as follows:

1 Start with A 4cm (1½in) below B.
2 Take A over then under B.
3 Double B in half and place across the collar points.
4 Hold B with thumb and index finger; drop A over.
5 Pull A through a little, then double A and pass behind, then through the hole in front.
6 Poke resulting loop through; even it out, then tighten.

THE GROOM'S WEDDING

The Four in Hand

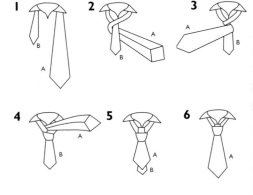

The Four in Hand

The Four in Hand should be tied as follows:

1 Start with A about 50cm (20in) below B.
2 Take A behind B.
3 Continue wrapping right round.
4 Pull A up through the loop.
5 Pull A down through loop in front.
6 Tighten.

The Windsor

1

2

3

4

5

6

The Windsor

The Windsor should be tied as follows:

1 Start with A about 60cm (24in) below B.
2 Take A behind B and up through loop.
3 Bring A over and behind B.
4 Take A down through loop again.
5 Then over and up through loop.
6 Bring through the knot and tighten.

What to wear

Ideally, the principal adult male members of the wedding party (including the bride's father) should all dress alike, although the groom may choose to be slightly different. To create the perfect coordinated look visit the outfitters with your best man, the ushers and, if possible, your father and the bride's father.

Hiring outfits

If hiring, you should book your clothes at least three months before the wedding, allowing time for alterations to be carried out, if necessary. It should be remembered that some weeks of the year will be busier than others and demand will consequently be higher. If your wedding date falls in this period, it may be necessary to book even earlier to avoid disappointment.

Lounge suit

The important thing at any event, and especially at your wedding, is to feel at ease. If more formal dressing makes you feel uncomfortable, then lounge suits are a good alternative. This is definitely a sharp and sophisticated choice, and while associated with register office weddings, is perfectly acceptable for religious weddings as well.

Coordinating colours

Should you (or the bride) be keen on creating a coordinated look, you can mix a lounge suit with any shirt and tie, which can easily be matched or contrasted with the wedding colour theme.

Shoes

The choice of shoes is also personal, although the rule is not to wear brown shoes with black trousers and vice versa. A well-fitting pair of leather shoes is your best choice, regardless of how comfortable your old trainers are.

Morning dress

The morning suit (penguin suit, top hat and tails) is usually worn for weddings before 3pm, and is still the most popular attire. The cut and style of the coat is very flattering to the majority of figures, and consists of a blue, black or grey tailcoat paired with matching or contrasting trousers, either plain or pinstriped.

Finishing touches

The outfit is completed by a white wing-collar shirt, a waistcoat of any colour, a cravat, a top hat and gloves (just held, not worn!).

Black tie

Black tie is traditionally worn for weddings later in the day or for those to be followed by a formal reception, and is ideal for a grand evening reception or summer ball. Obviously, if you're opting for black tie, you should inform your guests of this dress code, too.

A formal affair

You should wear a black dinner jacket, either single- or double-breasted, with ribbed silk lapels and no vents or covered buttons. Trousers should be tapered, suitable for braces and, officially, have one row of braid. The evening shirt, in cotton or silk, with either a Marcella or a pleated front, has a soft, turn-down collar.

Accessories

The bow tie is of black silk. Cummerbunds may be worn (with pleats opening upwards), but waistcoats are still much more acceptable. Black tie can be made as individual as you like with a colourful bow tie, matching waistcoat and pocket-handkerchief. Shoes should be black and well polished, and socks plain black.

White tie

One step smarter than black tie is white
tie. However, this is not usually worn
for weddings.

Frock coat

If you want to mark your wedding by wearing something really different, a popular choice is the frock coat, which is available in many colours and fabric designs. Usually made in beautiful brocade (or plain velvet), it looks great paired with a pair of plain black trousers and a wing-collar shirt and cravat.

Got the blues?

Many grooms in the armed forces choose to be married wearing their regimental uniform, which is not only ceremonial but also well suited to the traditions of a wedding. The traditional uniform for weddings is the Blues uniform: a blue jacket with a high collar, adorned with five brass buttons down the front and two on each cuff for officers.

Uniform

The jacket is teamed with matching blue trousers with a red stripe down the outside of each leg. No shirt is worn but the uniform is accessorized with a white belt and gloves. Military uniform may be worn by all grooms who are full time members of the armed services.

Traditional outfit

The best-known and most popular of these
is Highland morning or evening dress,
traditionally worn by Scottish grooms.
The kilt should be accompanied by a
Prince Charlie jacket or doublet,
a sporran, laced brogues, socks, bow tie,
and *sgian dubh* (a small dagger
carried in your sock).

Formal dress

Even if you're not having a traditional wedding ceremony, whatever your culture or religion you can still wear either the appropriate full traditional outfit or adapt various aspects of it to personalize any formal dress.

Beach wedding

If you're dreaming of sand between the toes, there's a whole range of options available. In the linen suit department there's everything from Man from Del Monte/Pierce Brosnan chic to *Miami Vice* crushed casual style. Just remember, light shirts, no ties, Panama hats optional. Or how about a custom-made silk suit?

Overseas advice

If you want to smarten up your act a bit,
a white tuxedo is great for overseas
weddings in hot climates. A white jacket
is best teamed with black trousers, a
white pleated-front evening shirt
and black bow tie.

The preparation

Get stuck in!

Some aspects of wedding planning, such as worrying about whether Uncle Fred's going to have a pop at the matron of honour now he's on Viagra, or whether the carpet will clash with the napkins, aren't much fun. But opting out is a bit like letting your mates plan your holiday – you can't complain when you end up in the Gulf rather than the Gulf Coast.

World wide weddings

In the enlightened Internet age in which
we live, weddings can actually provide an
excellent excuse for spending some time
on the computer. When she wails, 'I'll never
find a white Rolls Royce with pink suede
interior!', this is your chance to dash
off and search high and low – or just
on the confetti supplier directory – for
the solution to her problems.

Wedding web pages

Build your own website telling the world about the wedding — when, where, how, who and more. You don't need to know the first thing about website building to create a professional set of pages: cheats, beginners and those who know a good thing when they see it can head straight for the confetti wedding web pages to produce an easy-to-update site in about half an hour.

Food, glorious food

Many a groom has found his *raison d'être*
in the selection of food for the
wedding – known traditionally as
the wedding breakfast, regardless of
what time of day you consume it, and
even if it isn't bacon and eggs.

THE PREPARATION

Planning a feast

If your tastes lean towards the Michelin-starred end of the gastronomic spectrum, this is a great opportunity for you to have some fun in a good cause. If, on the other hand, you can't tell your sushi from your polenta, remind yourself (and your bride) that the wedding breakfast doesn't have to mean meat and two veg.

In the drink

Quite clearly, the drink goes with the food
(and the speeches, and the dancing…). So
it's a good idea for you to be on top of this
one, too. First, you need to decide whether
you're providing all the booze or only wine
for dinner and then a cash bar afterwards.
This needn't be impractical, even if you're in
a marquee – there are plenty of mobile
bars available for hire.

Drink orders

The usual choices are Pimms or Champagne for the reception before dinner, wine with the meal and then beer, spirits and wine afterwards. A good guideline for typical quantities is two glasses per guest for the reception drinks and then two or three glasses of wine during the meal. Don't forget to make bubbly available for the toasts.

Music choice

Whether you're having a band or a DJ,
the choice of music is important.
Build up a list of tunes you'd really like
to hear — and a blacklist of those you
wouldn't. Don't book a DJ without
first rifling quickly through his
CD collection to make sure
it's not all Bon Jovi.

THE PREPARATION

Play that funky music

Make sure the DJ has your playlist in advance, and get the best man to bring another copy to the reception so there can be no horrible Agadoo mix-ups.

Gift list secrets

There is no law decreeing that a gift list
must contain one vacuum cleaner, four bath
towels and eight tumblers. In fact, a gift list
is simply a chance for guests to give you a
'useful something' for married life, and if
you won't find a set of napkins useful, then
you don't need to have them.

Modern gift lists

Modern lists might consist of:

A complete shed full of DIY tools

Season tickets for your favourite team

A wine cellar

The honeymoon

Vouchers

A bathroom/conservatory

For tips on how to set up and tell people about alternative lists, see www.confetti.co.uk

The stag night

Although it's the task of your best man to make all the arrangements, if you have strong ideas on what you want to do – or definitely don't want to do – let him know firmly and early on. If you're short on ideas try www.confetti.co.uk for inspiration. Holding your stag night right before your wedding is to be avoided – give yourself time to recover!

Who pays?

Traditionally, the lads treat you to the big bash. But if you're keen on going somewhere pricey, you might want to let it be known that you don't expect them to foot the entire bill.

THE STAG NIGHT

Modern day stags

Increasingly, couples are holding combined
hen and stag nights, especially when the
majority of their friends are mutual.
Is it for you? That's for you and
your conscience to decide…

The dry run

It is customary – and highly advisable – for there to be a rehearsal of the ceremony shortly before the event. The celebrant will take you through your part in the ceremony and answer any questions.

Learn your lines

The rehearsal might inspire you to 'learn your lines', if you have not already done so. Although the minister usually asks you to repeat his words when the time comes to give your vows, learning the lines will enable you to deliver them with confidence. It's much more romantic to be gazing at your bride, than looking for a prompt from the vicar!

The night before

It is considered unlucky for the bridegroom to set eyes on the bride before the wedding ceremony, so even couples who live together tend to spend the night before their wedding apart.

Wedding morning checklist

- Do you have your buttonhole?
- Has the best man got the rings?
- Do you have your change of clothes for the next day?
- Has the luggage for your first night and honeymoon – including documents, tickets, passports – been delivered to your first night hotel or stowed in the car boot?

THE BIG DAY

Wedding morning checklist

- Do you have some spare change in case of an emergency?
- Do you have a crib sheet of events?
- Your speech notes?
- The thank-you gifts?
- Your going-away car keys, if you're driving?

Waiting game

At a church wedding, the bridegroom and the best man should arrive about half an hour before the service, to await the arrival of the bride, either in the vestry or seated in the front pew on the right-hand side.

THE BIG DAY

I do, I do, I do

At a given signal, the bridegroom takes his
place at the chancel step before the altar,
with the best man standing to his right.
Then your future wife will begin that
long, long walk up the aisle.

You may now kiss the bride

Once you are officially husband and wife,
with your bride on your left arm you
proceed to the vestry for the signing of
the register. After receiving congratulations
and greetings from both sides and when the
bride is ready, you again give her your left
arm and together you lead the bridal
procession down the aisle.

Civil ceremonies

Much the same procedure is followed in a civil wedding, which can be much simpler or just as ceremonious, depending on what you and the bride have decided.

Flash, bang, wallop

Be prepared to have photographs taken for up to an hour (or sometimes more) after the ceremony and during the first part of the reception.

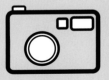

THE BIG DAY

At the reception

You should welcome your guests as they arrive at the reception and mingle with them, introducing your bride to any members of your family and friends whom she has not already met. Or you may stand in a formal receiving line to greet guests individually as they file into the dining area.

Speech!

The bridegroom is supposed to reply to the toast to 'the bride and groom', proposed by the bride's father. The primary purpose of your speech is to say thank you to the bride's parents for their daughter and for the wedding, and also to thank your parents and guests.

Cutting it

The cutting of the cake usually follows the last speech, which is traditionally the best man's. However, more and more couples choose to combine cake with dessert, and cut it before the speeches.

Shall we dance?

You may start the dancing with a romantic 'first dance'. After this you are free to enjoy your reception as you wish, but remember that you are one of the reasons people are there, so try to mingle.

Keeping with tradition

If you're being ultra-traditional, you and your bride will disappear at some point later in the evening to change, to then re-appear to say goodbye to your guests before 'going away' on your honeymoon.

All night long

If you plan to party until the bitter end, be polite and warn your older guests. They were brought up to think it rude to leave a reception before the bride and groom!

Plan ahead

Most couples don't follow the tradition of leaving their reception early to begin the honeymoon (why waste a great party?), so don't forget to book your first night's accommodation in a local hotel. You might want to plan a nice surprise such as candles, soft music, Champagne or flowers.

Gifts...

It is traditional for the bride and groom to present a gift to their mothers – usually flowers – during the speeches. This is in the spirit of 'thank you for being my mother', rather than a gift for anything they may or may not have contributed to the wedding.

More gifts...

It is also traditional for the bride and groom to exchange presents with each other on the day; the bridegroom also pays for the thank-you presents for the bridesmaids. Often this is jewellery, but it could be any kind of memento of the wedding day. You may also want to thank your best man and ushers. Often couples like to give them cufflinks to wear on the day. Find inspiration at www.confetti.co.uk

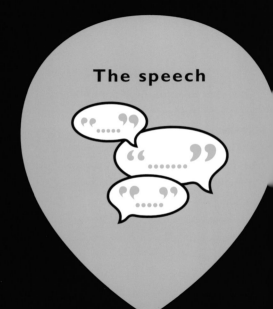

THE SPEECH

Traditionally, your speech comes between the father of the bride's and the best man's.

It offers you, as a couple, the opportunity to say your thank yous to all the people who have helped to make the wedding come together and to present them with gifts.

What to say

Your speech also gives you a chance to
reflect on the event that has brought
everyone together. You may well want to
talk about how you met your bride, relate
some funny and/or touching anecdotes
describing how the romance developed,
and perhaps say something about the
nature of love and marriage in general.

THE SPEECH

A joint message

If your bride is not making a speech,
remember that all your words should be
from both of you. Bear this in mind
throughout your speech – don't just include
your new wife as an afterthought! Oh – and
beginning your speech 'My wife and I...'
usually provokes some immediate
audience participation.

Speech checklist

Your speech is likely to include:

- Thanks to the father of the bride (and any other speakers) for their speeches. If he has expressed his faith in you (or said something similar), you might want to say something along the lines that you hope that you won't let him down/are proud to be his son-in-law etc.

THE SPEECH

• Some remarks about how successfully the wedding is going, perhaps drawing in some references to any amusing or striking incidents that have happened during the day.

THE GROOM'S WEDDING

Speech checklist

- Thank and offer presents to all the people who have helped with the wedding, including both sets of parents (especially the mothers) and the 'retinue': bridesmaids, ushers, page boys, flower girls etc. Include here mentions and/or gifts to anyone else you want to thank – dressmakers, performers, caterers etc.

Speech checklist

• Thank everyone for coming. Send good wishes to any guests who are too ill to attend etc.

Speech checklist

• Describe the background to the happy day. How did you and your bride meet? What were your first impressions – and hers? Who made the first move? Any other amusing or embarrassing stories (tip: the more humiliating to you, the funnier for everyone else!)

THE SPEECH

Speech checklist
- Say something exclusively from you to your bride about how happy you are to be marrying her and how much you are looking forward to your shared future etc.

Speech checklist
- Include a few words about the best man, perhaps pretending to dread what he is planning to say about you. This will help to introduce him to those guests who haven't met him before.

Speech checklist

- Conclude with a toast from you and your new wife to the bridesmaids.

Pre-speech jitters?

Remember, this is the best audience you will ever have. Why? Because from the moment you stand up to the moment you sit down, the entire audience is totally FOR you. The very reason you're standing up is because you are intimately connected with the people beside you — and so is the audience.

Coping with nerves

Whatever you say will be listened to and respected. Not only that, but guests listening to speeches often really want to laugh because it breaks tension and because they want to let you know they're with you. So be assured, even a vague attempt at a gag will be warmly received!

THE HONEYMOON

Traditionally, the groom plans the honeymoon and foots the bill as well – although most couples now simply share costs. There's a current trend for grooms to return to the tradition of 'surprise' honeymoons: Norman 'Fatboy Slim' Cook took new wife Zoe Ball on a mystery trip; and 'Big Breakfast' star Johnny Vaughan did the same for his bride.

Surprise honeymoon

If you do plan a surprise trip for your partner, make sure you have a good idea of her expectations and plan things you'll both enjoy doing. You'll also need to advise her on what clothes to pack (beach or city?) and ensure she has all the necessary documentation and vaccinations.

Careful planning

For many couples, on the other hand, sitting down together to plan the trip of a lifetime is one of the most exciting parts of the pre-wedding experience, and something they can do without family interference. So, perhaps you could take on the research and organization, but do the planning together.

Honest decisions

What do you BOTH want to do?
Make sure that neither of you is
agreeing to two weeks on a beach,
even though you've always hated
beach holidays, simply to keep the
other happy.

THE HONEYMOON

Do what *you* want

Remember, too, that you don't have to
follow other people's preconceptions
about what to do on your honeymoon.
'Whatever makes you happy' is truly the
key and worth bearing in mind. So, if playing
Scrabble together is what you really enjoy,
don't worry that it isn't romantic
enough – just do it.

'A quiet, relaxing time together – anywhere would do'

If all you're really after is time together and the stress of long-haul flights isn't your scene, then a cottage in Wales may serve you just as well as an expensive all-inclusive Far Eastern beach holiday.

THE HONEYMOON

'A little bit of luxury and privacy'
If you want something glamorous and gorgeous, then saving on travel expenses in favour of a top-class, exclusive location may be the best bet. How about flying low-cost to France — then staying in luxurious châteaux or hotels?

THE GROOM'S WEDDING

'Sun, sea and sand'

Walking hand-in-hand through the
Mediterranean surf on a white sandy beach
is surely the definitive honeymoon scene.
Just be sure – especially if you are active
types – that you really do both want to be
lazing around for all that time. You might
consider combining the tropical beach
with a week of...

THE HONEYMOON

'... action!'

An activity element – perhaps walking, skiing or cycling – can be perfect if you both love the activity involved. After all the stress of the wedding – and all that food and drink! – some decent exercise can be invigorating and restorative.

Final words of wisdom

Despite all that preparation and planning,
things do sometimes go wrong, but as long
as you're calm you'll be able to cope with
any little crisis that may occur.

Final words of wisdom

Above all, relax and enjoy it!
Don't forget this is *your* wedding
day; many grooms look back and
remember it fondly as the best
day of their lives.

ABOUT CONFETTI.CO.UK

Confetti.co.uk is the UK's leading wedding
and special occasion website, helping more
than 500,000 brides, grooms and guests
every month.

To find out more or to order your confetti
party brochure or wedding and party
stationery brochure,
visit: www.confetti.co.uk
email: info@confetti.co.uk
call: 0870 840 6060

Other books in this series include:
The Bride's Wedding
The Bridesmaid's Wedding
Your Daughter's Wedding
The Wedding Book of Calm